FISHING THE SHENANDOAH VALLEY

AN ANGLER'S GUIDE

Fishing

THE Shenandoah

Valley

M. W. Smith

University of Virginia Press

CHARLOTTESVILLE AND LONDON

University of Virginia Press

© 2004 by the Rector and Visitors of the University of Virginia

All rights reserved

Printed in the United States of America on acid-free paper

First published 2004

9 8 7 6 5 4 3 2 1

LIBRARY OF CONGRESS CATALOGING-IN-PUBLICATION DATA

Smith, M. W. (Michael W.), 1963–

  Fishing the Shenandoah Valley : an angler's guide / M.W. Smith.

   p. cm.

  ISBN 0-8139-2296-8 (pbk. : alk. paper)

   1. Fishing—Shenandoah Valley (Va. and W. Va.)—Guidebooks   2.

Shenandoah River Valley (Va. and W. Va.)—Guidebooks. I. Title.

  SH464.S53S65 2004

  799.1'09755—dc22

2004006878

All photographs by Dwight Dyke,

used courtesy of the photographer

Map by Chris Harrison

To my wife

How gallantly he comes along,

Pulls like a sailor long and strong.

Give him no particle of slack;

Hold steady, though the line crack.

The tension now is far too great,

For 'tis a bass of mighty weight.

—"AN ODE TO LAKE BASS,"

GEORGE J. SEABURY, 1890

Contents

Preface

Welcome to *Fishing the Shenandoah Valley: An Angler's Guide.* The Shenandoah Valley holds unique historical and geographical significance. The valley played a vital role in the Civil War, and witnessed many of its skirmishes. It is also home to Shenandoah National Park—established by Congress in 1926—and contains 80 miles of Skyline Drive which runs along its summit. Besides scenic overlooks, the park offers camping, fishing, horseback riding, hiking, nature trails, and bird watching. The Shenandoah Valley, which is generally considered to range from Waynesboro and Staunton in the south to Front Royal and Winchester in the north, is also home to the scenic river for which it is named. This book covers not only the Shenandoah Valley proper, but encompasses the entire Shenandoah River drainage, including the trout streams in the Allegheny Mountains to the west. Whether you are new to the Shenandoah Valley or a longtime resident, novice fisher or pro, this book will provide you with the information you need to enjoy the angling opportunities in the area and to catch more fish from its waters.

I begin, in chapter 1, by discussing fish species common to the streams of the Shenandoah Valley. These range from tiny native trout to three-foot-long muskie. Chapter 2 surveys native trout water in the Shenandoah National Park and covers, in detail and by county, many of the stocked trout streams listed by the Virginia Department of Game and Inland Fisheries (VDGIF). I offer suggestions on where and how to fish these waters, including both spinning and fly-fishing tactics and techniques.

Chapter 3 turns to Lake Frederick and Lake Shenandoah, the largest impoundments in the region. While warm water species such as largemouth bass, crappie, bluegill, and catfish dominate these lakes, walleye and muskie are also stocked. General instruction on how to access and fish each of these bodies of water (including winter fishing conditions), as well as contact information, is provided.

Chapter 4 offers detailed information on fishing the Shenandoah River, including float trips on the South Fork (in its entirety, from the VDGIF public boat ramp at Port Republic to the public landing at Front Royal) and on the Main Stem (from the confluence of the North and South Forks at Riverton to the West Virginia line). Entry and exit points are described in detail, together with useful tips about how to negotiate the river's rapids. I also discuss how to fish successfully during the winter and spring months when conditions become extreme. The Shenandoah River is well known for its excellent smallmouth fishing, but great largemouth bass, muskie, and catfish angling await as well.

In addition to all of this information, you'll find a comprehensive map of the Shenandoah Valley streams, notes on specific fishing locations keyed to maps in DeLorme's *Virginia Atlas and Gazetteer* (4th edition), and an appendix that lists local guide services, tackle shops, camping sites, lodging, and the like. In short, this book will tell you where, when, why, and how you will catch more fish in the Shenandoah Valley.

Safety must be your foremost concern when floating streams. Local canoe liveries (see the appendix, pp. 79–82) can provide you with advice concerning river condition and water hazards that may require portage, as well as necessary equipment and flotation devices. The following is the list of normal stream classifications for rating rapids that are used in trip descriptions throughout this book. If the temperature is below 50°F, or the trip extends through wilderness areas, the river should be considered one class more difficult than normal.

CLASS I: Slow-moving water with small waves and few obstructions. Easy rescue.

CLASS II: Moderate rapids with waves less than three feet high and wide channels that are obvious without scouting. Some maneuvering required. Rescue level of difficulty low.

CLASS III: Formidable rapids with high, irregular waves, often capable of swamping a canoe. Narrow passages that require complex maneuvering and scouting. Rescue difficulty high.

CLASS IV: Long, difficult rapids with constricted passages that often require precise maneuvering in turbulent waters. Waves capable of swamping an open canoe. Scouting from shore a necessity, and conditions make rescue extremely difficult.

CLASS V: Dangerous and violent rapids with highly congested routes that should always be scouted from shore. Not for open canoes. Rescue conditions hazardous, with significant danger to life.

CLASS VI: Difficulties of Class V carried to the extreme of navigability, making rescue nearly impossible. For teams of expert rafters only.

Acknowledgments

I am forever indebted to my wife, Beth, who not only fishes with me at times, but also indexes my books. Thanks also to others who spent time on the water with me: John Kemp (navigator/fisherman extraordinaire), Josh Parks, Steve Cahill, Lou Kalina (an excellent guide), and especially Sterling and Sarah Herbst of Massanutten, who also graciously offered their hospitality during the research for this book. And once again I wish to express my gratitude to everyone at the University of Virginia Press who makes this series possible.

FISHING THE SHENANDOAH VALLEY

Fish Species Common to the Shenandoah Valley

There are numerous species of fish in the Shenandoah Valley's lakes and streams. The following is a list of the more popular types of game fish you are likely to encounter.

Largemouth Bass

(Commonly called black bass.) The largemouth is dark greenish in color on top with a white belly. A series of black splotches extend laterally along its side, forming a horizontal line to its tail. It has a large mouth, with an upper jaw that extends from the corner of the mouth to the rear of the eyes. The dorsal fin is deeply notched. Citation size in Virginia is 8 pounds or 22 inches. Largemouth bass are found in local ponds, lakes, and streams, including a very healthy population in the Shenandoah River. Look for them in the coves and creek mouths of local lakes and along the banks of the Shenandoah where submerged vegetation, stumps, and logs are located. These fish are opportunistic feeders and will eat other fish, crayfish, snakes, frogs, and terrestrial insects. Spawning usually takes place from late April to early June. The best artificial lures include plastic worms, jigs, crankbaits, jerkbaits, spinnerbaits, and topwater varieties.

Rock Bass

(Also know as redeye.) This fish is a member of the sunfish family and rarely weighs more than 1 pound. It has a short stout body and a large mouth. Its back is green and sides can be somewhat golden colored, and each scale has a central black spot. Dark spots on the lower body form small stripes. This species is commonly caught by smallmouth anglers, who recognize its tendency to provide a ferocious strike with little fight to follow. Citation size in Virginia is 1 pound or 12 inches. Rock bass can be found in almost any stream with rocks and ledges in the Shenandoah Valley. They eat all forms of small aquatic and terrestrial life, including crayfish, minnows, and insects, and usually spawn during the same period as the black bass. The best artificial lures include jigs and spinners.

Smallmouth bass

Smallmouth Bass

(Also called bronzeback and smallie.) You can identify smallmouth by the coppery-brown color and greenish sides with dark vertical bars. Three dark bars radiate from the cheek across the gill cover; the upper jaw does not extend as far back as a largemouth's. Citation size in Virginia is 5 pounds or 20 inches. Smallies prefer cool clear water and bedrock ledges, which is why the Shenandoah River is one of the top smallmouth bass fisheries in the state. Crayfish, madtoms, hellgrammites, minnows, and aquatic insects make up most of their diet. Spawning normally takes place from late April to early June. The best artificial lures include jigs, spinners, jerkbaits, and topwater varieties.

Bluegill

(Also commonly called bream.) Bluegills are members of the sunfish family. They have dark blue or green backs that fade into a silvery, yellow-green side marked by five to seven vertical bars. The cheek area is usually bluish in hue, and has a large black spot (earflap) behind the gill. While bluegills can grow to be quite large—the state record weighed 4¾ pounds—citation size in Virginia is 1 pound. These fish will eat just about anything, including crickets, worms, small minnows, and other sorts of aquatic life. They are found throughout the state's waterways and are great fighters, which probably accounts for why so many anglers get hooked on fishing as kids by catching this abundant game fish. You will find bluegills in the Shenandoah River and in Lake Frederick, which offers the best panfish angling in the region. Bluegills spawn in late spring and early summer when the water temperature exceeds 70°F. The best artificial lures include poppers, Beetle Spins, and small soft-plastic insect imitations.

Channel Catfish

(Also referred to as a spotted cat.) Channel cats have a deeply forked tail and a spotted, dark silver-gray body. Citation size in Virginia is 12 pounds or 30 inches. This fish is generally a nocturnal feeder that wanders the bottom of the rivers and lakes in search of a variety of food sources, including crustaceans, fish, and carrion. It can be found throughout the rivers and lakes of the Shenandoah Valley, around rocky ledges and in deeper pools. The Lake Frederick record, set in 1997, is over 27 pounds! The best artificial lures include anything from jigs to crankbaits.

Crappie

(Also called speckled perch and papermouths.) There are two species of crappie—white and black. The latter is covered in black splotches and is more green on the sides, whereas the former tends to be more lightly spotted and silver-sided. Citation size is 2 pounds or 15 inches. Their diets consist mainly of minnows and small insects. These fish tend to congregate in submerged brush piles and fallen trees, which makes jigging for them a favorite technique of local anglers. Crappie spawn in early spring when the water is around 50°F and can be caught in the shallow regions of both Lake Shenandoah and Lake Frederick in the springtime. The best artificial lures include jigs fished on light spinning rods, doll flies, and small crankbaits.

Muskellunge

(Also referred to as muskie.) This fish is the largest member of the pike family. It is usually golden olive on its back and gray on the sides, with faint spots or blotches running vertically in a stripe-like pattern. It grows quite large, feeding off of other fish, small animals, and waterfowl. Citation size in Virginia is 15 pounds or 40 inches. Muskie, which prefer clear lakes with plenty of vegetation, are stocked in Lake Shenandoah and are also found in the Shenandoah River. The best artificial lures include big game plugs—both topwater and diving varieties—as well as large-bladed spinnerbaits.

Redbreast Sunfish

(Also called redbelly.) This member of the sunfish family is found in the Shenandoah River and its tributaries and is identified by the bluish stripes on its cheek and gill cover as well as a long black flap at the end of the gill plate. Redbellies feed on insects and small crustaceans and are commonly found along the banks and at the ends of pools. In spring they spawn in the small gravel beds along the shoreline. Sunfish must reach 1 pound or 11 inches to be a citation in Virginia. The best artificial lures include flies and small spinners.

Brook Trout

(Commonly known as brookie or mountain trout.) This fish species is native to the eastern mountains of the Appalachians and prolific in the creeks of the Shenandoah National Park. Its coloring is a spectacular blend of florescent purples and yellow and red spots with faint blue rings around them. The belly is white with distinct red-orange pectoral fins that sport a vertical black-and-white stripe. Citation size in Virginia is 2 pounds or 16 inches, but a 12-inch native is considered a bragging-rights fish by Virginia standards. These trout need clear cold cascading creeks with plenty of water flow and small pools. They spawn in the fall and feed mainly on aquatic insects and their larvae, as well as on various terrestrials. The best artificial lures include dry and wet flies, nymphs, and small in-line spinners.

Brown Trout

Brown trout were originally introduced from Europe. Their colors vary between olive and golden brown with red and brown spots on the sides. Large males often have a prominent hook-jaw feature and colorful orange bellies during the fall spawning period. Citation size in Virginia is 5 pounds or 25 inches. Insects, minnows, and crayfish comprise their diet. They can live in warmer and slower water than brook trout and have adapted well to the region's streams, establishing a thriving wild population. Browns grow large in bigger streams

Walleye

such as Mossy Creek. The best artificial lures include dry and wet flies, streamers, spinners, and jerkbaits.

Rainbow Trout

Distinguished by its silver sides, black spots, and long pink stripe, the rainbow trout can also grow quite large—citation size in Virginia is 4 pounds or 22 inches. They have been imported from the Rockies and are the mainstay of the stocking program in the Shenandoah Valley area. Rainbows spawn in the early spring months and like fast-flowing rivers as well as deep lakes. The best artificial lures include dry and wet flies, streamers, nymphs, and in-line spinners.

Walleye

Related to the sauger, and the largest member of the perch family, walleye are typically olive brown with golden-flecked sides. They grow to citation size at 5 pounds or 25 inches. These fish lie near the bottom of deeper holes in the river by day and move onto gravel sandbars and shallow ledges to feed at night on baitfish, leeches, and crawfish. Walleye are stocked in Lake Frederick, where fish up to 9 pounds are caught. I have also had success fishing for walleye in the Main Stem of the Shenandoah River, below the Warren Dam. The best artificial lures include jigs, jerkbaits, and crankbaits.

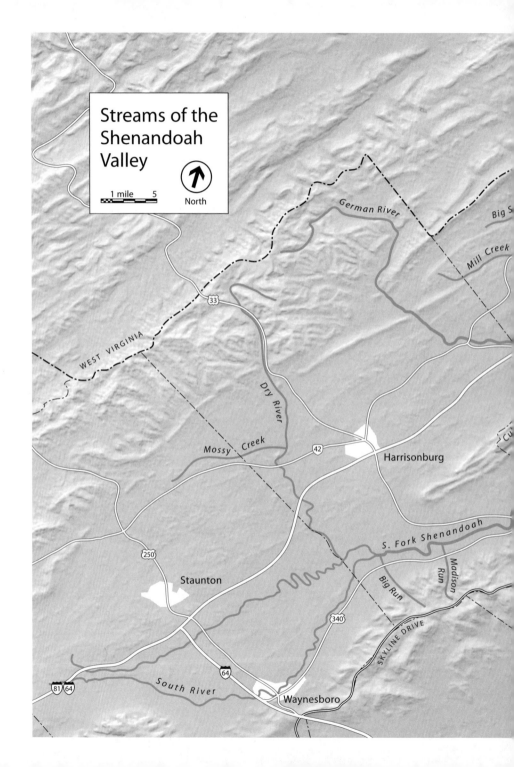

Streams of the
Shenandoah
Valley

1 mile   5

North

German River

Big S

Mill Creek

33

WEST VIRGINIA

Dry River

Cu

Mossy   Creek

42

Harrisonburg

S. Fork Shenandoah

250

Madison Run

Big Run

Staunton

340

SKYLINE DRIVE

81 64

South River

64

Waynesboro

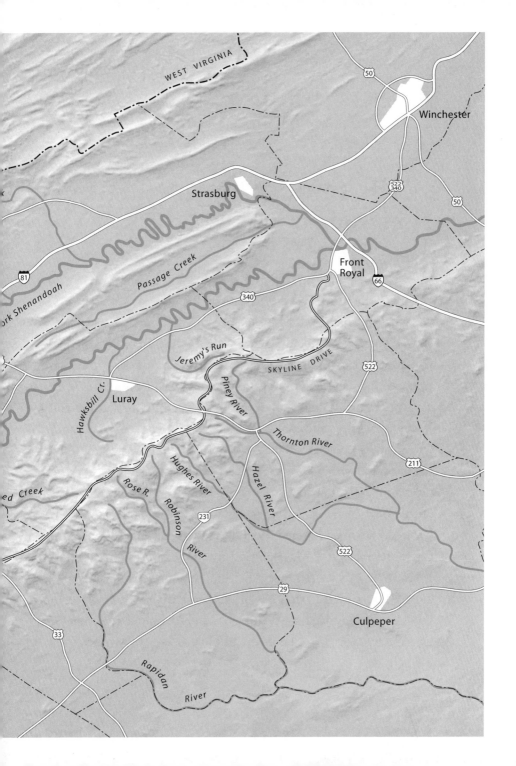

2

Fishing for Trout

Virginia maintains a relatively healthy population of both native and stocked trout species—brook, brown, rainbow, and golden among them. Shenandoah Valley residents—including those living in Staunton, Harrisonburg, Winchester, and Front Royal—are fortunate to have a wealth of both stocked and wild trout waters in close proximity. Wild trout populations (of which brook is the only native species) require cool, well-oxygenated water (often the familiar cascading pools of the "native" creek) and a clean creek bottom on which to lay eggs. These creeks are often canopied in rhododendron and difficult to access. There are numerous streams in the Shenandoah National Park that contain native brook trout, such as the well-known and popular Rapidan River (which is designated catch-and-release) in Madison County. Many of the native fish are in the 6- to 9-inch size range. All fishing in the Shenandoah National Park is restricted to single-hook, artificial lures only. The creel limit, on streams where harvesting of trout is allowed, is 6 trout per day, and the fish must be 9 inches or more in length. A 7-inch minimum size limit has been imposed on all trout creeled in Virginia. Since these streams aren't stocked, a special trout license is not needed—just a Virginia freshwater fishing license. To contact the Shenandoah National Park call (540) 999-3500.

Fishing in Shenandoah National Park

Although not always the case, the plethora of native trout streams in the park can generally be fished in a similar manner. Small in-line spinners (such as Joe's Flies) with modified single hooks can be used effectively to cast under overhangs and work the characteristically tight streams. In these settings, fly-fishermen will probably want to use shorter rods (7½ feet or less) and fine tippet (6x or 7x). There are excellent spring hatches of Quill Gordons and March Browns in the park. I have found dry-fly patterns such as Mr. Rapidans, Irresistibles, and Royal Wulffs to be most effective. Prince and Hare's Ear nymphs are good choices to try in the colder months and in the deeper runs. Above all, fish upstream whenever possible (employing roll casts to counter the underbrush and overhanging trees) and practice stealth to catch these wild brookies!

In the next few pages I list a majority of the more popular streams in the Shenandoah National Park (grouped by western and eastern slopes) and note the location of and directions to each. Since camping is allowed in the park, backpacking in from the trails on Skyline Drive and spending the night is a great way to fish the more remote sections of many of these creeks. By applying and adapting the aforementioned techniques to each of the individual

Float fishing from canoe

streams, you should have success catching wild trout in this extraordinary area.

Note that here and elsewhere throughout the book, each watercourse name is accompanied by a reference to the page on which it can be found in DeLorme's *Virginia Atlas and Gazetteer* (4th edition; see the appendix, p. 84).

Western Slope

Big Run (from Doyles River Parking Area on Skyline Drive)
VIRGINIA ATLAS AND GAZETTEER: 67

DIRECTIONS: This is probably the largest stream on the western slope, and access requires an arduous hike in and out from Skyline Drive at the Doyles River Parking Area (just south of milepost 81). Take the Big Run Loop Trail from the overlook about 2 miles down the mountain to Big Run Portal Trail, which leads to the river.

There is no bottom access to this stream, so you will have to come in from Skyline Drive. Though difficult, the hike in on Big Run Loop Trail is well worth it! Try attractor patterns and small nymphs for best success on this remote stream.

Jeremy's Run (top from Elkwallow Wayside Picnic Area on Skyline Drive/bottom from VA 611 near Rileyville)

VIRGINIA ATLAS AND GAZETTEER: 74

DIRECTIONS: Also one of the larger western slope streams, and thus a popular fishery, Jeremy's Run can be reached via a steep hike from the top at Skyline Drive (park at the Elkwallow Wayside Picnic Area—milepost 24), or from the bottom, near Rileyville, off VA 611 (which parallels the stream). To get there, take U.S. 340 south from Front Royal and turn left onto VA 662 at Rileyville after you cross the stream, and then right onto VA 611. Follow this until you cross the stream again.

Fishing access is sketchy at the bottom due to the proximity of private landowners in the area. I suggest that you access this stream from Skyline Drive at Elkwallow Wayside.

Madison Run (at Browns Gap Parking Area on Skyline Drive/
bottom from VA 633 in Grottoes)
VIRGINIA ATLAS AND GAZETTEER: 67
DIRECTIONS: This relatively small stream can be reached from Skyline Drive at Browns Gap Parking Area (milepost 83), or from the
bottom off VA 663 in Grottoes. Grottoes is located between
Elkton and Waynesboro on U.S. 340. Park at the end of VA 633
when you reach the gate and follow the forest service road up the
stream.

This is a fine creek that gets better (as do most in the park) the
farther up you go. Resist the impulse to fish the bottom runs, as the
plunge pools increase in number and quality as you ascend the
service road.

Naked Creek (East Branch from Naked Creek Overlook on Skyline
Drive/West Branch from VA 607)
VIRGINIA ATLAS AND GAZETTEER: 67
DIRECTIONS: This creek flows out of the park near the town of Shen-
andoah. There are three branches—South, East, and West. The only
access to the East Branch (and Naked Creek Falls) is via Skyline
Drive from the Naked Creek Overlook at milepost 53; bear in mind,
however, that no trailhead exists. To reach the West Branch take
U.S. 340 south from Shenandoah to VA 609 (Naked Creek Road)
and turn left. Follow this road (which turns into VA 759) until you
reach VA 607, which bears to the left and dead-ends partway up the
West Branch, where parking is available.

You will find beautiful, fishable water right from the start on
Naked Creek. Fish your way up from the bottom, where some nice-
sized brookies reside. Try an Adams dry fly.

Eastern Slope

Hazel River (upper part from Hazel Mountain Trail off Skyline
Drive/bottom from VA 600)
VIRGINIA ATLAS AND GAZETTEER: 74
DIRECTIONS: Hazel Mountain Trail, off of Skyline Drive between
mileposts 33 and 34, allows access to the upper part of the stream.
To reach the bottom, from U.S. 522 near Sperryville, take VA 231
south to VA 608. Turn right and follow to VA 600. Turn left and go
about a mile to gate.

There is good fishing in the upper reaches of this small stream
accessible via White Rocks Trail and Hazel River Trail (which leads
to Hazel Falls).

Hughes River (top from Shaver Hollow Parking Area on Skyline
Drive/bottom from Nicholson Hollow Trail parking lot near Nethers)
VIRGINIA ATLAS AND GAZETTEER: 74
DIRECTIONS: The Hughes can be reached from the Shaver Hollow
Parking Area on Skyline Drive between mileposts 37 and 38. Follow
the Corbin Cabin Cutoff Hollow Trail about a mile and a half to the
Nicholson Hollow Trail, which parallels the stream. The lower part
can be reached from a parking lot for the Nicholson Hollow Trail
near Nethers. To get there, from U.S. 522 near Sperryville, take VA

231 south for about 6 miles, then turn right onto VA 707 and follow until you cross the creek. Turn right again and follow a short distance to Nethers, where you will bear left onto VA 600 (which leads to the trail).

The Hughes is a popular stream that is not hard to reach from the bottom near Nethers or from the top off of Skyline Drive. If the parking lot is full, you may want to try your luck on Brokenback Run, its major tributary. To reach it, go left at the parking area for the Hughes.

North Fork, Thornton River (from Thornton River Trail Parking Area on Skyline Drive/bottom from VA 612)

VIRGINIA ATLAS AND GAZETTEER: 74

DIRECTIONS: To reach the North Fork, park at the Thornton River Trail Parking Area between mileposts 25 and 26 on Skyline Drive and take the trail that leads to the stream. To access the stream from the bottom at Sperryville, take U.S. 522/211 north to VA 612. Turn left and follow up the river.

You can fish the Thornton River along U.S. 211 west of Sperryville, and nearby you will find a great fly shop that takes is name from this stream (see the listing for the Thornton River Fly Shop in the appendix, p. 82; call for seasonal operations).

Piney River (from Piney Branch Trail off Skyline Drive/bottom from VA 612)

VIRGINIA ATLAS AND GAZETTEER: 74

DIRECTIONS: This feeder creek of the Thornton River can be accessed via Piney Branch Trail, either from Skyline Drive at milepost 22 or from the bottom via VA 612 near Sperryville. From Sperryville, take U.S. 522/211 north to VA 612 and turn left. Then turn right onto VA 600 and follow until you find (limited) parking at the trail.

Once a little-known gem, this stream has become popular recently due to its mention in some prominent national magazines. As with all the fine trout streams in the park, fishing pressure has had an impact.

Rapidan River (upper reaches from Milam Gap Parking Area on Skyline Drive/lower stretches in Rapidan Wildlife Management Area)

VIRGINIA ATLAS AND GAZETTEER: 68

DIRECTIONS: To access the upper reaches off the Skyline Drive, go to the Milam Gap Parking Area at milepost 53 and take the Mill Prong Trail. To reach the lower stretches of the river take U.S. 29 south from Madison and turn onto VA 230 west. Then go right onto VA 662 at Wolftown, and finally bear right again on VA 662 at Graves Mill. This will dead-end with parking at the end of the road in the Rapidan Wildlife Management Area. The trail leads you to Big Rock Falls, near Camp Hoover, below which the Laurel Prong and Mill Prong join to form the Rapidan.

This is probably the most popular stream in the park due to its size and quality habitat. The Rapidan was a favorite stream of President Herbert Hoover, and even has a fly named after it! While there is good fishing through the Rapidan Wildlife Management Area, the two prongs above Camp Hoover are worth the hike as well.

Fly-fishing on the Robinson River, near Criglersville, Madison County

Robinson River (from Whiteoak Canyon Parking Area on Skyline
Drive/bottom from VA 600)

VIRGINIA ATLAS AND GAZETTEER: 74

DIRECTIONS: From Skyline Drive, park at the Whiteoak Canyon
Parking Area between milepost 42 and 43 and take the trail that
runs down to the river. To reach it from the bottom on U.S. 522 at
Sperryville take VA 231 south and turn right onto to VA 670 at
Banco. Then turn right onto VA 600 just past Criglersville; this road
follows the stream up the mountain to the park boundary and the
trails that lead to Whiteoak Canyon and Cedar Run Falls. There are
parking areas on the left.

You can access the Robinson along VA 600 above Criglersville for
about 4 miles until you reach its headwaters—the tributaries of
Whiteoak Run and Cedar Run. To reach the parking areas for these
from the bottom see the directions above. To reach Cedar Run from
Skyline Drive, park at Hawksbill Gap on Skyline Drive near milepost 45 and take Cedar Run Trail to the stream. To reach Whiteoak
Run from the top, park at milepost 45 and take the forest service
road down to the stream.

Rose River (top from Dark Hollow Falls Parking Area on Skyline
Drive/bottom from VA 670)

VIRGINIA ATLAS AND GAZETTEER: 74

DIRECTIONS: To reach it from the top, park at the Dark Hollow Falls
Trail Parking Area between milepost 50 and 51. Follow the trail
down Hogcamp Branch to the Rose River Falls. To get to the bottom, from U.S. 522 at Sperryville take VA 231 south and turn right
onto VA 670 at Banco. Follow this road for about 3 miles until you

reach the end. There is a parking area at the park boundary, and a forest service road follows the stream for a mile or so.

The Rose is a dandy little stream full of wild trout. If the winter fishing gets tough, try a Mr. Rapidan nymph on the Hogcamp Branch, a feeder to the Rose that can also be reached from the top parking area.

Stocked Waters by County

There are approximately 600 miles of stocked trout water in Virginia available for fishing, and over one million fish are stocked annually (from October through June), according to Virginia Department of Game and Inland Fisheries (VDGIF). A Virginia trout fishing license is required on these waters, as well as a National Forest stamp when you are fishing within its boundaries. *Note:* From June 16 through the month of September anglers can fish in stocked waters without a trout license.

The following streams in and around the Shenandoah Valley are traditionally stocked by the VDGIF. The list is not exhaustive: One notable exclusion is Little Passage Creek, a category C stream in Shenandoah County. A phone number has been set up for you to check the latest stream stockings by county before you plan a trip: (434) 525-FISH (3474). Stocking schedules and other information can also be obtained online at www.dgif.state.va.us/fishing/stock/troutstock.cfm.

These are the stocking categories according to the VDGIF trout stocking listing; note that they are subject to change:

CATEGORY A: Stocked once in October, November/December, January/February; twice in March, April; once in May.

CATEGORY B: Stocked once in November/December, January/February, March; twice April 1 through May 15.

CATEGORY C: Stocked three times between October and April.

H: Stocked for Trout Heritage Day (first Saturday in April).

DH: Delayed Harvest; catch-and-release only October 1 through May 31.

NSF: Waters do not receive fall and early winter stockings.

Madison County

Hughes River (Category A; from VA 601)

VIRGINIA ATLAS AND GAZETTEER: 74

DIRECTIONS: From U.S. 522 at Sperryville, take VA 231 south for about 6 miles to VA 707, then turn right and follow this dirt road until you cross the stream and reach a hardtop (VA 601). The stream is stocked along VA 601—upstream to the town of Nethers and downstream to VA 231.

This fast-flowing, freestone stream with long runs and formidable pools is easily accessible from the roadside. I have waded along the road here and the traffic can be surprisingly heavy, so be careful while unloading. My best luck came from probing the deeper pockets with Pheasant Tail nymphs.

BIG FISH TIP *Fly-fishermen should try Hare's Ear nymphs during the winter months and Adams dry fly in the summer.*

Robinson River (Category A; from VA 670)

VIRGINIA ATLAS AND GAZETTEER: 68

DIRECTIONS: From U.S. 522 at Sperryville, take VA 231 south to Banco and turn right onto VA 670, which runs north along the river to the confluence with the Rose—a bridge at VA 600. Parking is also available here.

Stocking signs are visible all along the stretch above the town of Criglersville. Right below the bridge where the Rose and Robinson meet is a long, deep hole and a good starting point for fishing up or down the stream. I worked this area in the winter months with large nymphs shortly after a winter stocking but found no holdover trout willing to take a fly. I had better luck farther upstream and on its sister tributary, the Rose River.

Rose River (Category A; from VA 670)

VIRGINIA ATLAS AND GAZETTEER: 68

DIRECTIONS: From U.S. 522 at Sperryville, take VA 231 south to Banco and turn right onto VA 670, which takes you along the river above its confluence with the Robinson.

This is a designated Heritage Day stream—a throwback to the opening day of trout season (traditionally the first Saturday in April). There is a nice holding pool for stocked trout at a spillway just below Graves Mountain Lodge. I caught some nice rainbows here on egg patterns after meeting an older gentleman on the bank who held up a fine stringer of fish he had taken on salmon eggs.

BIG FISH TIP *Salmon eggs are a great choice for trout after a winter stocking.*

Spin-cast fishing on the Robinson River, near Criglersville, Madison County

Page County

Cub Run (Category B; George Washington National Forest)
VIRGINIA ATLAS AND GAZETTEER: 73
DIRECTIONS: Located in the George Washington National Forest on Massanutten Mountain. Take U.S. 340 north from the town of Grove Hill to VA 685 and turn left. Go about a mile until you reach the dirt road on the left that leads into the George Washington National Forest. This road runs along the creek upstream for a couple of miles where the run is stocked.

This high-gradient, small creek is a tributary of the South Fork of the Shenandoah River. Some of the better fishing is found at the bottom of the stocked area, downstream of the remnants of two old furnaces. Spinners work well in the swift spring flow. My wife, Beth, and I worked our way up through this stretch of beautiful trout water with fly rods during a Christmas Eve snowstorm—a memorable trip, although we failed to land a trout.

BIG FISH TIP *Fly-fishermen should try black or white bead-headed Woolly Buggers.*

Hawksbill Creek (Category B; Luray-Hawksbill Greenway Park)
VIRGINIA ATLAS AND GAZETTEER: 74
DIRECTIONS: Hawksbill Creek is stocked in the town of Luray. You can gain access at the U.S. 211/340 intersection, at the Luray-Hawksbill Greenway Park.

This is a medium-sized stream that is easy to reach and should not be passed up if you are in the Luray area. Parking is available at both ends of the greenway on either side of Luray.

BIG FISH TIP *Try fishing downstream of the U.S. 211 bridge.*

Upper Passage Creek (Category C; George Washington National Forest)

VIRGINIA ATLAS AND GAZETTEER: 73

DIRECTIONS: From Luray, follow the public boat landing signs from U.S. 340 until you cross the Shenandoah River. Then take VA 675 north up Massanutten Mountain until you reach the George Washington National Forest signs and Caroline Furnace Camp Retreat. Turn left onto Forest Service Road 274, which parallels the creek from there. Stocking signs are visible. Bathrooms and parking are located at the Lions Trail Parking Area about 1 mile up the road.

I fly-fished this remote creek in the dead of winter and spotted a number of large rainbows holding in a gin-clear pool near the snow-covered trail. Unfortunately, these wary fish turned their noses up to everything I threw at them that day! After an hour of trying nearly every pattern in my flybox, I left them to match wits with the next fisherman.

Rockingham County

Dry River (Category B; George Washington National Forest)

VIRGINIA ATLAS AND GAZETTEER: 66

DIRECTIONS: Take U.S. 33 west of Harrisonburg for about 7 miles until you come across this stream within the George Washington National Forest boundaries; it continues to be accessible along the road to the West Virginia line.

The Dry River provides the nearby city of Harrisonburg with excellent stocked and wild trout fishing. I have caught brook trout up to 10 inches here using pink Hare's Ear nymphs. Try attractor patterns such as orange-colored Stimulators in the summer and caddis imitation nymphs in the winter. The stocking starts at the City of Harrisonburg Recreation Department–sponsored park, which is on the left above Rawley Springs. As you venture farther

Fly-fishing—rainbow trout

upstream, the river splits and is joined by a number of feeder creeks that are worth the effort to fish.

BIG FISH TIP *Try nearby Hone Quarry Run, another stocked creek in the George Washington National Forest off VA 257. There is an RV camp- ground/picnic area at the top and a stocked lake (Hone Quarry Lake).*

German River (Category C; George Washington National Forest)
VIRGINIA ATLAS AND GAZETTEER: 72–73
DIRECTIONS: From I-81, take VA 259 north/west about 10 miles to VA 820 and turn left, then go up to VA 826 and turn left again. There is easy access here since the road parallels the creek.

This is a shallow, heavily wooded mountain stream typically found in the George Washington National Forest. Try size 14 to 18 olive Elk Hair Caddis in the spring when hatches are obvious and Pheasant Tail nymphs when fish are not actively surface feeding.

BIG FISH TIP *Live-bait fishermen should try Blue Hole (off VA 820); there is a parking area and bathroom facilities are provided.*

Mossy Creek (Special Regulation—Fly-Fishing Only; Augusta County)
The accessible fishing section of Mossy Creek is actually in north Augusta County, extending 4 miles upstream from the Rockingham County line.
VIRGINIA ATLAS AND GAZETTEER: 66
DIRECTIONS: From I-81, take the Mt. Crawford exit north of Staunton and follow VA 257 to Bridgewater. Then take VA 42 south to VA 747

and turn right. The upper parking area is on the right at the bridge. To reach the lower access, continue down VA 747 a mile and turn left onto VA 613 at the church.

Mossy Creek is one of Virginia's premier, fly-fish-only, trophy trout streams to which a number of special regulations apply. First, you may park only at designated areas at the top and bottom reaches of the permissible fishing water. Second, no wading is allowed. And third, anglers may keep only one trout over 20 inches. Prior permission must be obtained in writing from the Virginia Department of Game and Inland Fisheries (see the listing in the appendix, p. 79). This spring-fed, limestone creek is considered one of the best trout streams in the state. Quality brown trout up to 6 or 7 pounds (originally released as fingerlings by VDGIF) can be caught here! Most fish are in the 12- to 16-inch range, however.

Mossy Creek is notorious for its finicky fish. The swift, clear springwater flows through open pasture in Augusta County, where approximately 4 miles of access is available. There is little gradient and few riffles, which makes presentation a key to effective fly-fishing. When fishing dry flies on Mossy, I like to use 9-foot leader with up to 5x tippet (just in case a huge brown hits) and make casts upstream as far as possible, allowing for a drift that won't "line" the fish. Approach the creek with care, keeping an eye for rising trout, and then match the hatch they are feeding on. In the springtime, it's a good bet that actively feeding brown trout can be fooled with Sulphur mayfly patterns. One of my favorites this time of year is a size 14 to 18 Yellow Sally. In the summer, I like to use terrestrials such as Dave's Hoppers and standard ant patterns.

BIG FISH TIP *Slowly drag dark-colored, size 4 to 6 Woolly Buggers through the silt along the bottom for those big browns.*

North Fork, Shenandoah River (Category B; near Broadway)
VIRGINIA ATLAS AND GAZETTEER: 73
DIRECTIONS: From I-81, take VA 259 north, which parallels the river past Broadway and permits great access for about 5 miles.

There is superb trout fishing in the headwaters of this scenic stream. Try size 10 to 14 green and black Woolly Buggers and streamers. The stocking starts just past Cootes Store and continues intermittently up the river until the German, a stocked feeder to the North Fork. The North Fork is big and bold through here and a real pleasure to fish with a spinning or fly-rod. I covered this stretch during a snowstorm one February and failed to catch a fish, yet I was thoroughly impressed by the water.

BIG FISH TIP *Also try nearby Shoemaker River, another tributary of the North Fork of the Shenandoah River. To get to it, turn off VA 259 onto VA 612 south.*

South River (Category A in Grottoes; Special-Regulations Delayed Harvest (DH) Waters in Waynesboro—Augusta County)
VIRGINIA ATLAS AND GAZETTEER: 67
DIRECTIONS: To reach the put-and-take water take U.S. 340 to Grottoes; to reach the special-regulations water in Waynesboro, from U.S. 340 take the Second Street bridge over the river to North Park, where the creek is easily accessible.

I fared well in early November right at the park, fishing a number of fine runs with a pink Hare's Ear nymph and catching rainbows up to 12 inches. There is a nice path along the right side of river, going upstream from the park. The special-regulations water extends 2.5 miles upstream to the Rife Loth Dam. This large stream has clear, deep water with ample riffles and runs. Try size 16 to 20 Blue Wing Olives in the spring and fall and size 14 to 20 dry Adams and Adams Parachutes in the summer.

BIG FISH TIP *Constitution Park in downtown Waynesboro hosts the annual Virginia Fly-Fishing Festival in April every year.*

Shenandoah County

Mill Creek (Category B; near Mount Jackson)
VIRGINIA ATLAS AND GAZETTEER: 73
DIRECTIONS: Take the VA 730 exit off I-81 near Mount Jackson. Then take U.S. 11 north until you reach VA 263 at Mount Jackson.

The stream is stocked along VA 263 west of I-81. There are some waterfalls and a spillway that provide a good habitat for trout. This medium-sized stream (25 feet wide on average) is nice for spinning or fly-rod enthusiasts to explore. Easy parking is available.

Peters Mill Creek (Category C; George Washington National Forest)
VIRGINIA ATLAS AND GAZETTEER: 74
DIRECTIONS: Located in the George Washington National Forest on Massanutten Mountain. Take VA 55 from I-81 at Strasburg and go

south/east until you reach VA 678. Turn right and follow about 10 miles to VA 758, then turn right. Follow until you reach Forest Service Road 273 at the creek.

This is a feeder stream of Passage Creek, best fished with a 2 to 3 weight fly-rod and 7x tippet or ultralight spinning tackle and Joe's Flies or small Rooster Tails.

Passage Creek (Category A; near Massanutten Mountain)
VIRGINIA ATLAS AND GAZETTEER: 74
DIRECTIONS: Take VA 55 from I-81 at Strasburg and go south/east until you reach VA 678. Turn right onto VA 678 south near Waterlick. This road parallels the stream along the top of Massanutten Mountain.

Passage Creek is a beautiful freestone stream with low gradient and easy access. The put-and-take section is part of the Heritage Day program. *Note:* The creek is designated delayed harvest (DH; single-hook, artificial lures only, catch-and-release from October 1 to May 31) for 1 mile downstream of the Warren County line.

Stony Creek (Category A; from VA 690)
VIRGINIA ATLAS AND GAZETTEER: 73
DIRECTIONS: From I-81, take VA 42 south at Woodstock and turn right onto VA 675 at Columbia Furnace. Follow this to VA 717 and veer left; then turn left again at VA 690 to fish the upper reaches of Stony.

This swift, high-gradient stream flows from the mountains of the George Washington National Forest near West Virginia. You could not have designed a more enticing East Coast trout stream than the upper Stony. You will find long runs that sport deep, limestone-shelved holes filled with turquoise water. Fly-fishers should try size 16 to 20 Mr. Rapidan and Royal Wulff and Pheasant Tail nymphs. I fished this stream on a frigid day in early spring using Woolly Buggers and nymphs but was amazed to catch only one fish, and a nice smallmouth bass at that!

BIG FISH TIP *Try its major tributary, Little Stony—a wild trout stream. Special regulations apply to the portion of the stream located within the George Washington National Forest. Forest Service Road 92 crosses the lower portion of the special regulations section. To reach it, turn right onto VA 608 from VA 675.*

Fishing Lake Frederick and Lake Shenandoah

While the Shenandoah Valley is home to numerous streams and creeks that serve as tributaries to the North and South Forks of the Shenandoah River, it also contains a few small public lakes that provide anglers with opportunities to stillwater fish for a variety of species, including smallmouth and largemouth bass, walleye, muskie, catfish, bluegill, and crappie. These lakes are each easy to reach and offer both bank fishing and concessions (bait, tackle, and other goods and services) to the public.

Lake Frederick

VIRGINIA ATLAS AND GAZETTEER: 78

DIRECTIONS: Lake Frederick is located 6 miles north of I-66 at Front Royal on U.S. 340/522. Turn left onto a paved road at the sign designating public fishing and travel a short distance to the lake.

This beautiful 117-acre lake in Frederick County is owned by the Virginia Department of Game and Inland Fisheries (VDGIF), and

Fishing for largemouth bass

is therefore free of any development along its banks. According to the VDGIF's 2002 *Freshwater Fishing Guide* (a good general reference that is updated annually), this is the best lake in Region IV for largemouth bass fishing. Recent sampling indicates that fish in the 2- to-4-pound range are most common, with some fish weighing up to 10 pounds! The current regulations in effect on the lake require that anglers return all fish between 12 and 18 inches. There is a creel limit of 5 fish per day, of which only one may be over 18 inches.

Lake Frederick is made up primarily of two deep coves and drops to 55 feet at the dam near the boat launch. Remarkably, the water remains unstained year round; when flooding in the valley in the summer of 2003 prevented anglers from fishing the rivers elsewhere, I found Lake Frederick to be gin clear. It is worth noting that a number of artificial reefs consisting of discarded Christmas trees and old tires are located strategically throughout the lake and provide a good habitat for both bass and crappie. Target these areas in the winter months with deer-hair jigs tipped with live minnows. You will have to locate these sunken refuges with your depth finder, and then anchor off them and jig vertically. This sort of fishing can be tedious, and fish may bite only for an hour or so during the middle of the day as the water temperature warms. There is also excellent shoreline cover surrounding the lake, including a forested bank, flooded timber, and lots of aquatic vegetation—perfect for casting buzzbaits for largemouth bass both early and late in the day during the summer months. The lake offers excellent bluegill and catfish angling opportunities as well—in fact, channel cats over 20 pounds have reportedly been caught by fishermen. Moreover, sustained walleye-stocking efforts in recent years have increased both population and catch rates, resulting in fish in excess of 5 pounds being taken. Facilities at the lake include a handicapped-accessible pier, concessions, and a boat ramp (electric motors only). Lake Frederick is open 24 hours a day, 7 days a week; contact the concession area (called Wolfs Minnow Bucket) for information on lake conditions at (540) 869-1104.

Lake Shenandoah

VIRGINIA ATLAS AND GAZETTEER: 67

DIRECTIONS: Lake Shenandoah is located east of Harrisonburg on VA 687, 2 miles south of U.S. 33. From I-81, take the U.S. 33 exit east at Harrisonburg. Go about 4 miles and turn right onto VA 687, which will take you to the lake.

This generally shallow, 36-acre lake in suburban Rockingham County, near Elkton and Harrisonburg, is being rehabilitated after years of sedimentation problems led to stunted fish growth. An organization called the Lake Shenandoah Preservation Association has assisted the Virginia Department of Game and Inland Fisheries in creating a hiking trail and placing benches around the lake. The trail allows bank fisherman ready access to all but the southern shoreline, which is steep and heavily wooded.

According to the VDGIF, sunfish, crappie, and largemouth bass are abundant. Muskie are also stocked in the lake, and with plenty of fish to prey on, these predators are growing to trophy size. Chan-

Lake Shenandoah, near Harrisonburg, Rockingham County

nel catfish up to 15 pounds have also been caught by anglers here. Some of the best fishing is near the dam at the lower end of the lake, where the water reaches 25 feet in depth. Facilities include a concrete boat ramp (electric motors only), concession/bait shop, and sites for bank fishing.

4

Fishing the Shenandoah River

The Shenandoah River is comprised of three stems—the North Fork, the South Fork, and the Main Stem. The North Fork is generally smaller and more shallow than the South Fork and has limited access, although fishing can be quite good in some of the more remote areas due to the seclusion and lack of pressure. The river as a whole is tranquil in comparison to its western cousins, the New and the James, with higher gradients and harsher rapids to navigate. The Shenandoah (which derives its name from a Native American term meaning "Daughter of the Stars") flows gently through the valley, crossing shallow ledges and creating numerous riffles along the way that provide excellent habitats for fish.

For most fishermen and -women, the year during which I wrote this book will be remembered as the year of the floods on the East Coast. Others will simply recall the months of poor fishing. Following two years of drought, in 2003 the Shenandoah River often ran at a volume of over 4,000 cubic feet per second (by comparison, normal summer flow is well under 2,000 cubic feet per second). Muddy water and high stream flows can make river fishing difficult, and it can become discouraging when hard-spent days on the water yield few fish. While many folks simply retire the rod and reel for weeks at a time, this in not always an option for fishing guides. On the Shenandoah, guides and anglers alike were forced to find ways to catch fish under these adverse conditions. While some were less successful than others, my clients at Greasy Creek Outfitters actually recorded more citation (trophy) fish that year than ever before.

When the river is up and colored, the first thing to realize is that to attract strikes you will have to go with bigger baits that create a larger profile and displace more water. In some cases, this means that you sacrifice numbers for size of fish. (This is usually fine with most folks!) You will also need to bulk up the tackle to accommodate larger lures. That is, you may need to go from 6-pound to 8-pound test on spinning outfits so that you can throw heavier soft plastics than you would normally use in the summer months. For example, I usually fish the Shenandoah with ⅛-ounce lead heads in my tube jigs during the summer, when water flow is typically lower, but switch to ¼-ounce when the river is high. The reason for this is simple: When the water is flowing at a higher volume, you need to use heavier jigs to get down to and stay in the strike zone. This is vital, since the strike zone will decrease due to low visibility. Color is also an important consideration when visibility is diminished. Usually the best contrast to brown or dingy water is a dark blue or purple bait; try 4-inch tubes (Case Salty Tubes are my favorite) in black neon.

An excellent lure for these conditions is the spinnerbait. Again, I bulk up this bait when fishing high and/or stained water. For example, I normally throw a ¼-ounce Neal's spinnerbait or buzzbait in the summer months when the water is lower than usual, but will go to a ⅜-ounce lure when the water is high. Chartreuse colors and large willow-leaf or hammered chrome blades are good choices. These lures not only get into the strike zone quickly but can be easily slowed to stay there. Spinnerbaits are most effectively fished off the shoreline, along islands and grass beds, or behind surface boulders where eddies form. Make sure to cast directly to the bank. The biggest mistake my clients make is short-casting to the bank—in effect, hitting the fish on the back with the lure. It is imperative to cast beyond the ambush point for the fish and retrieve into that zone if you want to have success in high waters.

Another great lure choice in high waters is the versatile crankbait. Long-billed crankbaits allow you to go deep quickly in swift water, even in midriver where fish may be holding on ledges 10 to 15 feet down. I have also had incredible success casting shallow-running crankbaits off the shoreline when the water is up. For color choice, I prefer "firetiger" when the Shenandoah is stained. One standby crankbait that I use when the water is high and dingy is probably sitting in your tackle box too—the Rebel Crawdad. This little bait has caught everything from big smallies to monstrous muskie for me. It will allow you to target riffles and shallow shelves best but can also be effective when used along the shoreline.

While both forks of the Shenandoah River contain an abundance of game fish species—the most prominent being smallmouth bass—the river has a reputation for an overpopulation of small bass (under 12 inches). Subsequently, the Virginia Department of Game and Inland Fisheries has implemented a 14- to 20-inch slot limit for black bass on the South Fork between Shenandoah Dam and Luray Dam. All fish within that range must be released, and only one fish larger than 20 inches may be harvested. This special regulation is also in effect on the Main Stem of the river from the Warren Dam downstream to the U.S. 17/50 bridge. The rest of the Shenandoah River, including the North Fork, falls under an 11- to 14-inch slot regulation—all fish within that range must be released. Jet motors are popular on the Main Stem, where fishing for bass, bluegill, catfish, and muskie is good and larger fish can be expected. *Note:* The entire Main Stem of the Shenandoah is under a health advisory for PCB contamination, and fish caught should not be consumed. For a map of Shenandoah River float trips, contact the Virginia Department of Game and Inland Fisheries (see the appendix, p. 85).

North Fork

The North Fork of the Shenandoah is seen by most anglers primarily as a wading stream—simply due to the fact that public boat landings are few and far between. There are only five public launch accesses, averaging roughly 20 miles apart. The North Fork also suffers from low water flow in the summer, which makes it difficult to float. Moreover, there are six dams and several low-water bridges to negotiate. The first dam is above Timberville; three are located between Edinburg and the VA 758 bridge east of Woodstock; and

Fly-fishing, North Fork, Shenandoah River, Rockingham County

two smaller dams are located between Strasburg and Riverton. Two that should be noted as presenting especially difficult portages are Chapman Dam, downstream from Edinburg, and the dam at Burnshire's Bridge, near Woodstock.

When fishing and floating, you should estimate approximately 1 mile per hour under good flow conditions. Low water levels, such as the North Fork is prone to have, require extending that rate of travel time. Because of this, float trips on the upper end of the North Fork will require that fishermen seek permission from landowners to camp along the river. Two floats on the lower end of the North Fork (between Strasburg and Riverton) are short enough to be made in one day. Wade fishermen can access the river at all of the public landings listed below and even farther upstream at various informal pull-offs along VA 259, above the town of Broadway. This area offers anglers opportunities to catch both trout (which are stocked above Cootes Store) and bass, especially in the spring when water levels are higher.

Largemouth bass, smallmouth bass, rock bass, sunfish, and bluegill are prevalent throughout the North Fork. Catfish and muskie are also present in the lower reaches. All black bass are protected by an 11- to 14-inch slot limit on the North Fork. There is also a health advisory due to the presence of PCBs downstream of Passage Creek.

The following section lists the five official Virginia Department of Game and Inland Fisheries public landings on the North Fork and directions to reach them:

Meems Bottom (canoe access only, VA 730)

VIRGINIA ATLAS AND GAZETTEER: 73

DIRECTIONS: The Meems Bottom launch is located directly off I-81, on VA 730 near Shenandoah Caverns. Limited parking is available here.

Chapman's Landing (concrete ramp, Willow Grove)

VIRGINIA ATLAS AND GAZETTEER: 73

DIRECTIONS: Chapman's Landing is located on VA 672 at Willow Grove, just off U.S. 11, south of Woodstock. From I-81, take VA 42 east to U.S. 11. Go south on U.S. 11 about 2 miles until you see VA 672 and the public boat landing signs on your left.

Strasburg (concrete ramp, City Park in Strasburg)

VIRGINIA ATLAS AND GAZETTEER: 74

DIRECTIONS: This landing is located at City Park in Strasburg, on VA 55. Turn onto Park Road from VA 55 and follow the public boat landing signs to the launch. This is a beautiful park that allows excellent wading access to the river. The float from Strasburg to Riverton makes for a long one-day fishing trip (approximately 10 miles). *Note:* There are two small dams to portage around on this junket.

Catlett's Landing (canoe access only, near Front Royal)

VIRGINIA ATLAS AND GAZETTEER: 74

DIRECTIONS: Catlett's Landing is located on the northern shore of the river near Front Royal. Take VA 637 north/west off U.S. 340 to

VA 626 and follow the public boat landing signs to the launch. There is a small pier at the landing available for use by bank fishermen. This launch can be used to break the Strasburg to Riverton trip in half.

Riverton (concrete ramp, in Front Royal)

VIRGINIA ATLAS AND GAZETTEER: 74

DIRECTIONS: The Riverton landing is located in Front Royal, off VA 637 downstream of the U.S. 340/522 bridge. There is a spillway directly above the ramp that requires a portage on river left, should you plan to use the launch as a take-out. This launch is just half a mile above the confluence of the North and South Forks of the Shenandoah and can serve as a put-in for the first float trip on the Main Stem, covered on pp. 67–70.

South Fork

The South Fork of the Shenandoah River has for years been popular with residents of the region and anglers from Northern Virginia and Washington, D.C., primarily due to its proximity to populous areas and the fact that it is chock-full of both largemouth and smallmouth bass. And there are lots of quality fish to catch as well. Spring is the best time to target big bass with chartreuse and/or white spinnerbaits and dark-colored plastic jigs, while fly-fishermen will want to cast large streamers of various sorts early in the season. Buzzbaits, in-line spinners, and pumpkinseed tube jigs are a good bet in the summer. For the fly-rod, try foam bugs such as Chernobyl Ants or variations of Chocklett's disc bugs, dead-drifted in swift runs with nearby drop-offs, especially in June and July. Try topwater plugs in the late summer and early fall for smallies as well. Good redbreast sunfish, channel catfish, and muskie fishing can be found throughout the river, but most especially in the bigger ponds at its many dams.

From the town of Shenandoah to Luray, a special regulation 14- to 20-inch slot limit exists, while for the remainder the limit is 11 to 14 inches. No fish within that size range may be kept. There is also a health advisory for mercury contamination placed on the upper end of the South Fork from Port Republic to the Page/Warren County line and for PCBs downstream from the VA 619 bridge near Front Royal. Overnight camping on national forest land is permitted; contact the Lee Ranger District at (540) 984-4101 for locations.

Largemouth bass

The South Fork of the Shenandoah has relatively mild rapids to navigate (a handful of Class IIs at normal levels), and thus little arduous paddling is necessary. However, four dams do require portage. The first is just above Island Ford (portage on left); the second is at the town of Shenandoah (portage on right); the third is upstream of the Newport access (portage on right); and the last is at Luray, a few miles above the Inskeep landing (portage on left). There are numerous liveries and outfitters throughout the valley (see the appendix, pp. 79–82) that can provide you with equipment and information about river and fishing conditions.

The following list of float trips includes locations of, and distances between, all the public landings on the South Fork of the Shenandoah. *Note:* You can compute travel time for fishing at approximately 1 mile per hour.

Port Republic (gravel ramp, off VA 955) **to Island Ford** (gravel ramp, off VA 642)

DISTANCE: 10 miles

VIRGINIA ATLAS AND GAZETTEER: 67

DIRECTIONS: (1) *Put-in at Port Republic.* From I-81 at Harrisonburg, take the U.S. 33 exit to Elkton; then go south on U.S. 340 to Grottoes. The put-in is 1 mile west of the intersection of U.S. 340 and VA 659 at Grottoes, off VA 955. (2) *Take-out at Island Ford.* From I-81 at Harrisonburg, take the U.S. 33 exit to Elkton; then go south on U.S. 340 until you reach the intersection of U.S. 340 and VA 649 and turn right. The take-out is off VA 642 under the VA 649 bridge. To reach it from the put-in, backtrack on U.S. 340 to VA 649 and turn left.

According to Lou Kalina, a local river guide (see the listing for Lou's Guide Service in the appendix, p. 80), the upper Shenandoah is a great place to fish early in the year for citation-sized smallmouth. In fact, Lou reports that there is other excellent water in the South Fork farther above this float, but you need permission to gain access to the river through private land. As good as the fishing can be, this float from the first public access on the South Fork is not favored by most fishermen, primarily due to the remnants of an old dam near the end of the trip. Also be aware that the upper South Fork is narrow and paddlers should always be on the lookout for strainers—areas where the river is apt to force your vessel into the bank and under overhanging trees.

The bridge at VA 708, near Lynnwood, allows informal access about one-third of the way through the trip (should you want to make just an evening's getaway or simply avoid the McGaheysville Dam section of the trip), but this is private land and permission should be sought out first. Floaters will find good fishing for the next couple of miles below the bridge, including a Class I rapid whose riffles provide a good summer habitat, but the water is slow from there to the island above McGaheysville Dam, a couple of miles above take-out. CAUTION: The remains of this old hydroelectric dam present paddlers with debris and dangerous hydraulics and should be portaged on the left side. The take-out is a gravel ramp on the right side of the river under the VA 649 bridge. *Note:* Village Store Canoeing (see the appendix, p. 82) is located near the put-in at Port Republic.

Island Ford (gravel ramp, off VA 642) **to Elkton** (canoe access only, under U.S. 33 bridge west of U.S. 340)

DISTANCE: 7 miles

VIRGINIA ATLAS AND GAZETTEER: 67

DIRECTIONS: (1) *Put-in at Island Ford.* From I-81 at Harrisonburg, take the U.S. 33 exit east to Elkton. Then go south on U.S. 340 from Elkton until you reach VA 649 and turn right to VA 642. The put-in is off VA 642 under the VA 649 bridge. (2) *Take-out at Elkton.* From I-81 at Harrisonburg, take the U.S. 33 exit east to Elkton. The take-out is under the U.S. 33 Business bridge, just west of the intersection with U.S. 340 in Elkton.

This is a great float! The intermittent riffles and deepwater ledges that characterize this stretch create ideal smallie habitats. The first rapid on river left at a small island (actually an old mill race) can be avoided by following the river's natural course to the right. Fishing is good below the rapid. Farther downstream is a Class I–II rapid with a pronounced ledge, offering some fine smallmouth fishing below it for a mile or so. Lou Kalina likes to use Neal's jigs in the spring to target big smallies through this part of the river. The color choice varies depending on water levels and clarity, he says.

Merck Park, on the right near the end of the float, allows informal boat access off Fourth Street in Elkton, but keep in mind that the gates close at dark. There is plenty of good water between here and the take-out, however, that you won't want to skip. Note that the island at the very end of this float must be taken on the right to make the take-out at the U.S. 33 Business bridge at Elkton (you will first cross under the bridge). CAUTION: There is a dangerous strainer on river right just past the first bridge where the current pushes paddlers under a large willow tree. I know of a number of people who have run into trouble here! Beware of midstream obstacles here as well.

BIG FISH TIP *Try white soft-plastic jerkbaits and bone-colored small crankbaits on this float early in the summer.*

Elkton (canoe access only, under U.S. 33 bridge west of U.S. 340) **to Shenandoah** (concrete ramp, off VA 602)
DISTANCE: 7 miles
VIRGINIA ATLAS AND GAZETTEER: 67
DIRECTIONS: (1) *Put-in at Elkton.* From I-81 at Harrisonburg, take the U.S. 33 exit east to Elkton. The put-in is under the U.S. 33 Business bridge, just west of the intersection with U.S. 340 in Elkton. (2) *Take-out at Shenandoah.* From I-81 at Harrisonburg, take the U.S. 33 exit east to Elkton, then turn left onto U.S. 340 north until you reach VA 602 in the town of Shenandoah. Turn left and follow until you reach the public landing, which is on the left before crossing the river.

This is a good trip for anglers who want to target both largemouth and smallmouth bass. Overall, I have not been very impressed with this float since the fishing action is generally slow. Still, a few riffles offer good angling near the middle of the trip, where some bluffs rise above the river's right shoreline. Try dead-drifting Case Magic Stiks in the slower water on this float. Texas rig these without any weight, making them essentially weedless, and cast them along wooded shoreline, under tree overhangs, and into downed timber. Allow them to sink and drift at the same rate as the current moving your vessel—then hang on! Sometimes bass will hammer these baits, while at other times the line will just feel "mushy."

Note: Slow water above the dam requires paddling at the end of float to reach the public boat ramp. Unfortunately for fishermen, this area is often overrun by jet skis and small recreational boats in the summer.

Shenandoah (gravel ramp, off VA 602) **to Grove Hill** (gravel ramp, on VA 650)

DISTANCE: 8 miles

VIRGINIA ATLAS AND GAZETTEER: 67/73

DIRECTIONS: (1) *Put-in at Shenandoah.* From I-81 at Harrisonburg, take the U.S. 33 exit east to Elkton, then turn left onto U.S. 340 north. Follow to the town of Shenandoah and turn left onto VA 602. Turn right off VA 602 onto a feeder road at the dam, just before you reach the bridge that crosses the river. The put-in is at the gravel landing downstream of the dam. (2) *Take-out at Grove Hill.* From I-81 at Harrisonburg, take the U.S. 33 exit east to Elkton, then turn left onto U.S. 340 north. Follow to the town of Shenandoah and continue on to Grove Hill. Turn right onto VA 650 at the public boat landing sign on U.S. 340 near Grove Hill. The launch is approximately 1 mile farther on the left.

This float begins directly below the Shenandoah Dam. There is some very good water for the first half a mile below this that can be accessed by wade fishermen as well. I suggest trying this area in the spring when water is up and fish have migrated in this direction. Just after launching, be prepared to negotiate a difficult Class II rapid on the left side of the island that splits the river. (Consider portaging along the island.) Not far into the float you will encounter a very long stretch of slow-moving, deep water that can be worked with a plastic worm or crankbait along the west bank. The fishing begins to pick up once you pass through a riffle on river right and encounter a large island that should be run on its left side. There are some nice shallow-water shelves and a number of long runs and pools along the island that offer great fly-rod action. I have found it especially effective to drift a foam bug down the west shoreline side of these narrow runs, which inevitably yields a bass or two in the 12-inch range.

Downstream of this area the river turns to the right and narrows into a Class I rapid that has a nice pool beneath it. I've caught a number of respectable fish here, including one that broke tippet on a hookset when I used a small, white Clouser minnow. One thing that you notice on this float is an overabundance of small baitfish and minnows in the shallows and the rapids, which makes streamers a good choice for the fly-rod. The fishing is okay for the next mile or so but picks up at about the 3-mile point, where a large shelf creates a single Class I rapid followed by a very large hole that continually deepens for roughly 100 yards. Concentrate your casts on the right side of this area. Soon after the hole ends you will encounter an island and another Class I rapid that can be run easily on the right side, but watch for strainers, as the stream will pull you close to the bank.

South Fork, Shenandoah River, Page County

About a mile farther, you will reach a strong Class I–II rapid that should be taken on the left side. Once you pass this rapid the river bends to the left, and there is another long stretch of slow, deep water with some elongated ledges at the top. Fish the right bank, which is deeper. After passing through this area you will come into a very nice 2-mile-long continuous stretch of quality water marked by small ledges, some boulders, and riffles. I have taken numbers of decent smallmouth by using poppers on a fly-rod in this area. As you finish this part of the float you are greeted by an easy Class I rapid; then the river widens and you will encounter another mile or two of good underwater rock formations and deep pockets that hold lots of fish. Target largemouth and smallmouth bass with top-water lures here; Zara Spooks and Heddon Torpedos work very well. A solid Class II rapid sits in this middle of this stretch and must be run on the far left side. Be careful: Once you drop over the rapid there is a large rock waiting that must be avoided. Shortly thereafter you will pass under the U.S. 340 bridge and then negotiate a few more small rapids before you reach the take-out (Grove Hill Landing) on river right, off VA 650.

Since this area is close to Massanutten resort, don't be surprised to find yourself sharing the river with numerous other groups of floaters—perhaps even an entire Boy Scout Troop!

BIG FISH TIP *Fly-fishers should dead-drift foam disc bugs through riffles and in chutes or across ledges.*

Grove Hill (gravel ramp, on VA 650) to Newport (gravel ramp, off U.S. 340)

DISTANCE: 6 miles

VIRGINIA ATLAS AND GAZETTEER: 73

DIRECTIONS: (1) *Put-in at Grove Hill.* From I-81, take the New Market exit east onto U.S. 211 toward Luray. Turn right onto U.S. 340 south and follow this route to Grove Hill. The put-in is on VA 650 a mile downstream of U.S. 340 bridge; turn left onto VA 650 at the public boat landing signs on U.S. 340 near Grove Hill to reach it. (2) *Take-out at Newport.* From I-81, take the New Market exit east onto U.S. 211 toward Luray. Turn right onto U.S. 340 south and follow this route to Newport. The take-out is off U.S. 340 at Newport.

The river near the Grove Hill landing presents mostly shallow runs and slower pools, creating an excellent area for wade fishermen, who can access the river along VA 650 for the first couple of miles from the put-in. Downstream, Massanutten (or Newport) Dam begins to back up the water about a mile upstream of the Newport access, calling for a difficult portage on the right. In the spring, local anglers use large spinnerbaits to catch hefty 3- to 4-pound largemouth bass in this area.

If you prefer to start the float below the dam, you can access the river—for a fee—via VA 617, off VA 650 (Waterside Drive). The fishing can be good below the dam, but there are a number of obstacles to watch for here (including the remains of a mill) that form a difficult Class II rapid and a steep drop-off near the end of the trip! I recommend a cautious approach and portaging along the island located to the left of the rapid.

BIG FISH TIP *Probe the deeper pockets with large tube jigs.*

Newport (gravel ramp, off U.S. 340) **to Alma** (gravel ramp, below U.S. 340 bridge) **to White House** (concrete ramp, below U.S. 211/340 bridge on VA 646)

DISTANCE: 3 miles to Alma; 9 miles from Newport to White House

VIRGINIA ATLAS AND GAZETTEER: 73

DIRECTIONS: (1) *Put-in at Newport.* From I-81, take the U.S. 211 exit at New Market east toward Luray. Turn right onto U.S. 340 south and follow this route to Newport. The put-in is located off U.S. 340 at Newport. (2a) *Take-out at Alma.* From I-81, take the New Market exit east onto U.S. 211 toward Luray. Turn right onto U.S. 340 south. Then turn left onto U.S. 340 Business (toward Luray). The take-out sits below the U.S. 340 Business bridge at Alma. (2b) *Take-out at White House.* From I-81, take the New Market exit east onto U.S. 211

toward Luray. Continue until you cross the river and turn left at the public boat landing sign onto VA 646. *Note:* Riverside Camping at Newport rents canoes (see the appendix, p. 78).

The upper trip boasts numerous ledges and Class I rapids that provide great fishing. At the start, you will find an area of submerged rocks that afford great cover for good-sized smallmouth and a good shoreline habitat for largemouth bass. A Massanutten resident, Sterling Herbst, and I boated a number of smallmouth bass through here in early April using blue 5-inch Case Salty Tubes and dark-skirted spinnerbaits with gold Colorado blades. Farther downstream, a series of riffles and a long rapid offer some excellent smallmouth fishing. These can be fished effectively with spinning or fly-rods. Some nice ledges sit just upstream of the take-out, which is on the right under the U.S. 340 Business bridge.

The first couple of miles of the second leg of this trip offer a diversity of good smallmouth habitats, including pools, runs, riffles, and ledges. About a mile into the float you will encounter the first of a series of islands, which are good areas to target in the spring while water levels are high. Probe the downstream breaks or eddies and the inside slews of islands in the spring for big fish. Sterling hung into a monster bass here that pulled drag and broke free as it broke the surface with his jig.

This trip also holds some deceptive Class I+ rapids that form large wavefields during high flow periods. I have encountered waves in excess of 2 feet that can soak the front paddler on this float. Be prepared for this if you are fishing early in the year, when air temperatures are low. The take-out is on right side of the river, at the U.S. 211 bridge.

BIG FISH TIP *The Rebel or Bagley's Crawdad with a red belly is an effective choice for spring smallies on this trip!*

White House (concrete ramp, below U.S. 211/340 bridge on VA 646) **to Massanutten** (concrete ramp, on VA 615) **to Inskeep** (concrete ramp, past Bixler's Ferry bridge on VA 675)

DISTANCE: 4 miles to Massanutten; 7 miles from White House to Inskeep

VIRGINIA ATLAS AND GAZETTEER: 73/74

DIRECTIONS: (1) *Put-in at White House.* From I-81, take the New Market exit east onto U.S. 211 toward Luray. Turn left at the boat landing sign onto VA 646 once you cross the river. (2a) *Take-out at Massanutten.* From I-81, take the New Market exit east onto U.S. 211 toward Luray. From U.S. 211/340 turn left onto VA 615 north and follow the boat landing signs 3 to 4 miles to the launch. (2b) *Take-out at Inskeep.* From I-81, take the New Market exit east onto U.S. 211 toward Luray. Then follow the public boat landing signs from U.S. 211/340 by turning on VA 675 and traveling for about 5 miles to the bridge at Bixler's Ferry. The put-in is across the bridge on the west side of the river.

This 7-mile section of the Shenandoah River, which holds large pools that provide excellent muskie and channel catfish habitats, is probably best suited for johnboats. If you decide to float it, you will encounter Luray Dam about 2 miles upstream of the Inskeep access; this requires a difficult portage on left. For more than a mile above the dam you will have to paddle backwater; here largemouth are your best bet.

This is a great area to try your luck in the winter months when the fishing has slowed down on the river. Because the river is pooled up above the dam, the water temperature can rise significantly on sunny days. Just a few degrees can trigger a memorable winter strike. When fishing during colder weather, you will want to "size up" your soft-plastic jigs (4- to 5-inch tubes and grubs) and slow down the presentation so that the baits literally crawl along the bottom. Another tactic I use is dead-sticking white flukes, especially on rocky points and shoals where you might find baitfish schooled. More often than not, bass are located in the deeper eddies and holding on deeper ledges within the river channel during this time of the year. These places can be successfully targeted with crankbaits and suspended jerkbaits, such as Husky Jerks. The key is to work these baits as slowly as you can possibly reel them, often stopping for 10 to 20 seconds at a time on the retrieve once you have gotten the bait down into the strike zone. (In March of 2003 I fished with Captain Forest Pressnell, host of the syndicated show *The Outdoor Sportsman*. We filmed an episode on winter fishing in which we employed a tactic I successfully use on the New River, drifting ⅛-ounce deer-hair jigs tipped with 2-inch minnows across midriver ledges. While this technique was effective for catching both smallmouth and largemouth bass, our biggest fish—a 4-pound smallmouth—was caught on a clown-colored Smithwick jerkbait worked meticulously across a series of midriver ledges that clearly held fish.)

CAUTION: A low-water bridge that crosses the river just before the take-out at Inskeep presents a difficult challenge for canoeists. Approach the take-out from river left along the left side of a small island that splits the river as you near the VA 675 bridge at the end of the float. A short portage around the low-water bridge is necessary to reach the parking area.

Inskeep (concrete ramp, past Bixler's Ferry bridge on VA 675) **to Foster's** (concrete ramp, on VA 684)

DISTANCE: 9 miles

VIRGINIA ATLAS AND GAZETTEER: 74

DIRECTIONS: (1) *Put-in at Inskeep.* From I-81, take the New Market exit east onto U.S. 211 toward Luray. Then follow the public boat landing signs from U.S. 211/340 by turning onto VA 675 near Luray and traveling for about 5 miles to the bridge at Bixler's Ferry. The put-in is across the bridge on the west side of the river. (2) *Take-out at Foster's.* From I-81, take the New Market exit east onto U.S. 211 toward Luray. Then follow the public boat landing signs from U.S. 211/340 by turning onto VA 675 near Luray and traveling for about 5 miles until you cross the river and reach VA 684. Turn right onto VA 684 (Page Valley Road). Follow the river north along VA 684 for about 10 miles to the public boat landing. *Note:* Boats can only go downstream (and motor back up) due to a low-water bridge just above the launch.

The fishing on this float picks up once you pass through a Class I rapid (the aptly named Mill Dam Rapids, where the remains of an old mill dam rest near a small island). I suggest following a route to the right of the island, as some exposed steel rods lie to the left. If you choose to run the rapid, stay to the far left. Over the course of the next couple of miles the fishing is quite good. Try soft-plastic jerkbaits (Case Salty Shads) and Rapalas through the riffles that follow. *Note:* Since this area lies within the boundary of the George Washington National Forest, camping is permitted along the left shoreline.

As you near the end of this trip, you will pass through Bumgardner's Rapids—a long series of shelves that hold good numbers of eager fish and should be worked thoroughly with soft-plastic spider jigs and grubs in the spring and flukes in the summer. The rapids eventually give way to an area called "the shallows." I have done well in the willow-grass beds and riffles here using Neal's jigs and spinnerbaits when the river flow was high in early spring. The take-out follows the remains of an old Indian fish weir on river left. *Note:* Bealer's Ferry canoe launch (about 2 miles above Foster's Landing off VA 684) allows you another access to this part of the river. Shenandoah River Outfitters and Shenandoah Lodge (see the appendix, p. 81) are located on VA 684 between Bealer's Ferry and Foster's Landing.

Foster's (concrete ramp, on VA 684) **to Bentonville** (canoe access only, downstream of VA 613 bridge)

DISTANCE: 18 miles

VIRGINIA ATLAS AND GAZETTEER: 74

DIRECTIONS: (1) *Put-in at Foster's.* From I-81, take the New Market exit east on U.S. 211/340 toward Luray. Turn at the public boat landing signs onto VA 675 and travel for about 5 miles until you cross the river and reach VA 684. Turn right and follow the river north for about 10 miles along VA 684 to the public boat launch. (2) *Takeout at Bentonville.* From I-66, take the U.S. 340/522 exit south at Front Royal and follow U.S. 340 to VA 613 and turn right. The takeout is off VA 613 downstream of the low-water bridge. Alternative take-out: You can cut this float in half by taking out at Burner's Ford—off VA 664 (Carvell Road) which connects with U.S. 340 near Compton. Parking is limited. There are also a number of forest service boat ramps on river left, including a concrete ramp at Mile 13. *Note:* Camping is allowed in the George Washington National Forest, which is located on the left side of the river and can be reached by land via VA 684.

There are plenty of Class I and Class II rapids to contend with on this arduous trip. The first major challenge is Goods Falls, a mile-long section of rapids, riffles, and ledges that hold some fine smallmouth. Lou Kalina and I fished this stretch together one June after a period of sustained rain. The river was high and muddy, making for difficult fishing conditions. Having guided anglers on the Shenandoah for over a decade, Lou knows the best tactics to successfully target fish in turbid water. We hugged the shoreline in his NRS Otter raft, and by throwing mainly blue ¼-ounce Neal's jigs with black trailers we managed to land twenty or so fish that day, mostly largemouth bass. One positive side to fishing in tough conditions is that you have the river to yourself, a rarity during the summer months. Along the way that day, Lou pointed out a tremendous bald eagle's nest, large as a small automobile, sitting high atop an old sycamore tree on the river left.

About one-third of the way into this float you will encounter Compton Rapids—a Class II–III rapid, with standing waves, that should be scouted (and portaged if necessary) from above and can be run on right of center. CAUTION: Large boulders lie on the left side near the bottom of these rapids. Look for a high train trestle on river right as you approach them. There are some good camping areas both above and below the rapids in the national forest land on river left. In fact, there are a number of primitive, no-fee camp-sites along this part of the Shenandoah. The next couple of miles present only mild rapids until you reach the alternative take-out at Burner's Ford—a steep dirt path on river right. You may want to leave yourself some sort of marker here, as it is easy to miss this.

The fishing is quite good for the next few miles. There are under-water boulders and rock shelves that attract some nice fish. Follow-ing a slow, deep stretch of the river you will encounter an old dam that creates a Class I rapid that should be run center to right. Another Class I–II rapid soon follows with a steep ledge; this can be run on far left or far right. The Hazard Mill Campground and Haz-ard Mill Recreation Area are located a few miles farther down on the left bank. The river splits here and the right fork is the main branch (the left is old mill race). Ledges, small rapids, and a num-ber of small islands define the river. The final couple of miles of this float are generally flat, shallow water. The take-out is on river left, at

South Fork, Shenandoah River, near Rileyville, Page County

a low-water bridge. *Note:* Shenandoah River Trips and Down River Canoe Company are located at the Bentonville landing, as is the Low Water Bridge Campground, which provides toilets and showers (see the appendix, pp. 77, 79, and 82).

Bentonville (canoe access only, downstream of VA 613 bridge) **to Karo** (canoe access only, on U.S. 340) **to Front Royal** (gravel ramp, off Luray Avenue)

DISTANCE: 9.5 miles to Karo; 15.5 miles from Bentonville to Front Royal

VIRGINIA ATLAS AND GAZETTEER: 74

DIRECTIONS: (1) *Put-in at Bentonville.* From I-66, take the U.S. 340/522 exit south at Front Royal and follow U.S. 340 to VA 613 and turn right. The put-in is off VA 613 downstream of the low-water bridge. (2a) *Take-out at Karo.* From I-66, take the U.S. 340/522 exit south at Front Royal and follow U.S. 340 through the town. The take-out is on the east side of the river on U.S. 340 at Karo, off Chapman's Farm Road. (2b) *Take-out at Front Royal.* From I-66 take the U.S. 340/522 exit south at Front Royal and follow U.S. 340 through the town. The take-out is off Luray Avenue, where it meets the river. *Note:* Shenandoah River Trips and Down River Canoe Company are located at the Bentonville launch and Front Royal Canoe Company is located just south of Front Royal off U.S. 340 (see the appendix, pp. 79 and 82). These liveries provide canoe rentals and shuttles (even if you provide your own canoe).

Numerous ledges and riffles define this float and, as expected, allow for some great smallmouth angling. In fact, I experienced one of my best days ever of river fishing on this stretch of the South Fork in early June of 2003. A consummate angler, John Kemp of Roanoke, and I boated over 100 fish that day with at least half measuring over 15 inches. We caught a dozen smallmouth bass that weighed over 2 pounds each, with the largest reaching 4 pounds— all on Neal's spinnerbaits and buzzbaits!

The trip starts off with some shallow midriver ledges that hold fish; then the river begins to deepen after about a mile and you reach a long RV campground on the left. An excellent riffle lies along the right side of the river and some shallow ledges follow, offering outstanding fishing. Try running buzzbaits off the bank and out along these ledges—and be ready for a ferocious strike! John and I spent an hour paddling back upstream time and again to drift across this area. Past this, you will reach the Shenandoah River State Park (also called Andy Guest State Park; see the appendix, pp. 78 and 86) on your right; look for a gravel canoe launch where a small creek enters the river. There are a couple of canoe and tube "stairs" through the park that allow you to exit the river here. (The entrance to the park can be reached via U.S. 340; however a fee is required.) This area affords tube (and wade) fishermen good access to the river. Work the right shoreline at the bottom of the park with spinnerbaits and buzzbaits, and the shallower ledges and rapids in midriver with soft-plastic tube jigs and flukes.

A series of Class I rapids marks the bottom of the park, and then the river begins to widen over the next few miles, forming numerous islands and side channels. On that memorable June day, John and I caught fish in the 14- to 16-inch range off of the shallow water ledges above McCoys Ford—a long broad shoal split by islands. We targeted the right bank as we negotiated the ford's rapids until at length we reached the bottom, where John landed a beautiful 19-inch smallie! A further series of small rapids and deep water ledges mark the end of this stretch, and then a deep pool forms in the river above the Karo landing. The take-out at Karo is on river right along Gooney Run. To reach it you will have to paddle through a slot in an islet where the creek enters on the right.

The second section of this float begins shallow and rocky with the Class II Karo Rapids at the start; to avoid them, stay right. Below these you will find some good smallmouth fishing. Downstream there are some deep pools in the area know as Kings Eddy, near where the Front Royal Canoe Company operates its livery. This is a great area to pick up largemouth bass on Case Salty Tubes and Magic Stiks. You will encounter some riffles and small rapids the rest of the way until you cross under the VA 619 bridge. The take-out at Front Royal is on the right, next to a pumping station and cement walkway.

BIG FISH TIP   *Buzz it!*

Main Stem

The Main Stem begins at the confluence of the North and South Forks of the Shenandoah near Front Royal. Bass, bluegill, catfish, and muskie fishing are quite good, and large fish can be expected. Since the river is deeper here and more uniform in gradient—even flat in places—many anglers use jet motors. Although the Main Stem of the river is still as splendid as its two tributaries, you will, nonetheless, encounter signs of encroaching urban life from metropolitan Washington, D.C., as it spreads its influence into this area of the state. A 14- to 20-inch slot limit is in effect from the base of Warren Dam, near Front Royal, downstream to the U.S. 17/50 bridge. An 11- to 14-inch slot limit applies to the rest of the Main Stem. No fish within these ranges may be kept. *Note:* The entire Main Stem of the Shenandoah is under a health advisory for PCBs and fish caught should not be consumed.

Riverton (concrete ramp, off VA 637) **to Morgan's Ford** (gravel ramp, VA 624 bridge)

DISTANCE: 8 miles

VIRGINIA ATLAS AND GAZETTEER: 74

DIRECTIONS: (1) *Put-in at Riverton.* From I-66 at Front Royal, take the U.S 340/522 exit south and turn left onto VA 637 just before crossing the river. The put-in is on the North Fork downstream of the U.S. 340/522 bridge. (2) *Take-out at Morgan's Ford.* From I-66, take the U.S. 340/522 exit north at Front Royal; turn right onto VA 661 and follow this road to VA 624, then turn right again. This will take you to the low-water bridge on the east side of the river. CAUTION: The public landing at Morgan's Ford is located directly on the right shoulder of VA 624 and requires that boaters and canoeists blindly back across the busy road into the water to launch or load. In addition, this access point sits directly above the low-water bridge, which can create a dangerous situation for boaters launching here should they lose motor power; it may also present problems for canoeists who aren't careful as they approach the take-out.

Unless you are interested in a difficult portage around the Warren Hydroelectric Dam at about the midway point of the float, I don't suggest beginning at Riverton. If you do choose to make the entire trip, be aware that it includes paddling though long sections of flat water behind the dam, and that an arduous portage must be made on river left. Another put-in option is a ramp (still above the dam) at the public golf course (Front Royal Country Club) downstream from I-66, on VA 655. Use of this launch, however, requires an annual membership and fee. If you do paddle through the pond, be prepared to encounter lots of boat traffic, as the impoundment created by the dam is big enough to accommodate large ski boats and pontoons!

Many anglers opt, as I do, to take their jet boats from Morgan's Ford upriver to the dam and fish their way back down to the ramp (which entails navigating through the rapids in the Horseshoe Bend area—a couple miles below the dam). I have a 17-foot Grizzly Tracker with a 40 horsepower Mercury Jet Drive that is ideal for fishing the Main Stem. Such boats allow fishermen the luxury of working a particular stretch of the river carefully, without having to traverse the long distances that float trips often require. In this case, you can easily run the 3 miles upstream to the dam and fish the entire stretch of river in the evening after work.

The long pool below the dam is a great place to find big fish. There is a series of 3- to 6-foot-deep ledges along the right shoreline (as you face the dam) that should be worked meticulously. John Kemp and I were surprised to boat a 2-pound walleye through here on a summer trip in 2003. My guess is that this is the farthest point upstream in the Shenandoah River that walleye can travel from the Potomac River basin. John caught the fish on a daiquiri-colored Mister Twister grub, which proved to be effective throughout the entire day. The water was up and stained, as it had been for most of the season. Under these conditions, soft-plastic jigs and tubes are great baits for locating fish, especially where the water is moving.

Horseshoe Bend, an area of extended rapids downstream of the dam, was another place where we found consistent action. In fact, John caught about a dozen bass averaging about 1 pound each using Mister Twisters through this stretch of the river. The nicest fish we

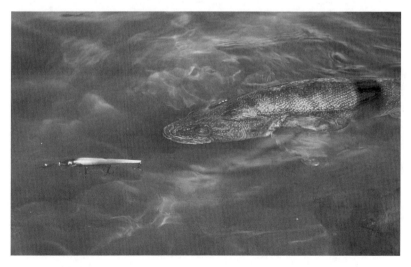

Fishing for walleye

boated, however, was a 16-inch smallmouth that succumbed to a Pop-R retrieved just above a shallow ledge.

The take-out is on the right side of the river at a low-water bridge. Be careful to approach the bridge along the river-right bank, or you may have difficulty making it to the launch. CAUTION: Low-water bridges can create dangerous hydraulics for boaters; proceed with care.

Morgan's Ford (gravel ramp, VA 624 bridge) to Berry's Ferry (concrete ramp, under U.S. 17/50 bridge)

DISTANCE: 11 miles

VIRGINIA ATLAS AND GAZETTEER: 74/79

DIRECTIONS: (1) *Put-in at Morgan's Ford.* From I-66, take the U.S. 340/522 exit north at Front Royal; turn right onto VA 661 and follow this road to VA 624, then turn right again. This will take you to the low-water bridge on the east side of the river. CAUTION: The put-in at Morgan's Ford is located directly off VA 624, below the one-lane bridge, which creates a dangerous traffic situation. (2) *Take-out at Berry's Ferry.* From I-66, take the U.S. 340/522 exit north at Front Royal. Follow until U.S. 340 splits from U.S. 522 to the east. Turn right and follow U.S. 340 until you reach U.S. 17/50. Turn right again and follow until you reach VA 622 on the left just before crossing the river; this road will take you to the boat launch.

The trip begins with a Class I rapid just below the low-water-bridge put-in at Morgan's Ford, so be prepared for it at the start. Shallow riffles, boulders, and ledges characterize the upper portion of the trip and create ideal smallmouth bass habitats for the next couple of miles; following this there is a set of Class I–II rapids that should be approached on the left side. After a mile or so of slow water you will reach Treasure and Hardin Islands (the latter is a mile long). This is an excellent area to work topwater baits and soft plastics in the summertime. Two of my favorites are Heddon Baby Torpedos and Case Salty Shads.

You will paddle through a few small rapids over the next couple of miles until you reach a final Class I rapid near the end of trip; this should be run through the channel in the middle of the grass beds from which it is formed. I have caught some nice bronzebacks in the run below the island using crankbaits and tube jigs. Below the rapid the river deepens and the banks are lined with blowdowns and submerged trees. Fish these with topwater baits early in the morning and late in the evening for largemouth bass. During the day, try flukes, Case Magic Stiks, and jigs for bucketmouths as well. The take-out is a steep ramp behind a small man-made jetty on river left, beneath the U.S. 17/50 bridge. *Note:* This ramp can present problems for the loading of boats.

Berry's Ferry (concrete ramp, under U.S. 17/50 bridge) **to Lockes** (concrete ramp, on VA 621)

DISTANCE: 10 miles

VIRGINIA ATLAS AND GAZETTEER: 79

DIRECTIONS: (1) *Put-in at Berry's Ferry.* From I-66, take the U.S. 340/522 exit north at Front Royal. Follow until U.S. 340 splits from

Spin fishing

U.S. 522 to the east. Turn right and follow U.S. 340 until you reach U.S. 17/50. Turn right again and follow until you reach VA 622 on the left just before crossing the river; this road will take you to the boat launch. (2) *Take-out at Lockes.* From I-66, take the U.S. 340/522 exit north at Front Royal to Berryville; turn right onto VA 7, then right again onto VA 608 and follow to VA 621. Turn right onto VA 621 when you reach the river. The launch is just a bit farther on the left. *Note:* To reach the take-out from the put-in, backtrack up U.S. 17/50 for about a mile to VA 621 (River Road) and turn right. This road mostly parallels the river and will lead you to Lockes Landing (about 6 miles). *Note:* The steep ramp at Berry's is tricky for boaters but no problem for canoeists. There is a man-made jetty at the bottom of the ramp that is supposed to help, but it can make matters worse when the current is high.

This excellent float is a favorite of local guides. In fact, I have encountered dories full of fly-fisherman casting popping bugs and Sneaky Petes on this trip. The fishing is outstanding from the start. Just below the put-in the river splits around Burwell Island; there is a small streambed that runs along the right, but the major flow is to the left. Stay with this and you will pass a small island that should also be run on the left side, and be sure to cast to the eddies along the way. A nice pool that forms at the base of the island is worth fishing as well. The waterway narrows some below here due to the splitting of the river, and you can practically cast to both shorelines from the middle. John Kemp and I employed this tactic when the water was high and dingy in 2003 by drifting the center of the river and tossing Bomber 6A and 8A crankbaits to opposite banks. This strategy paid off with some 12- to 15-inch smallmouth.

Crankbaits are a great lure choice when the river is up and dingy because they are so versatile and can cover a lot of water quickly. They allow you to go deep in swift water, even in midriver where fish may be holding on ledges 8 to 12 feet deep, and shallow-running crankbaits can be deadly when worked off the shoreline and over shoals. My favorite color in stained water is "firetiger," and an excellent choice anytime is the Rebel Crawdad in a similar color pattern. In fact, I was able to catch a number of nice fish that day on this lure.

Prime water—shallow ledges, large boulders, sunken timber, and deepwater riffles—follows. This is a great area for working soft-plastic flukes, jigs, and topwater baits. John Kemp picked up some nice fish here on a Mister Twister grub by carefully casting the jig behind midriver structure.

Below Burwell Island you will enter into a long outside bend on river left (called Calmes Neck) that is followed by a mile of intermittent Class I rapids. This is a great place to work streamers on a fly-rod or to use a large Mepp's Algea or Rooster Tail spinner. As you near the end of the float you will notice (also on river left) a number of rough put-ins on the private property along VA 621, which parallels the river on the left bank all the way to the take-out at Lockes Landing.

BIG FISH TIP *Try an orange and brown Bandit crankbait.*

Lockes (concrete ramp, on VA 621 off VA 608 south of Berryville) **to Castleman's Ferry** (concrete ramp, on VA 7 east of Winchester at bridge)

DISTANCE: 5 miles

VIRGINIA ATLAS AND GAZETTEER: 79

DIRECTIONS: (1) *Put-in at Lockes.* From I-66, take the U.S. 340/522 exit north at Front Royal to Berryville; turn right onto VA 7, then right again onto VA 608 and follow to VA 621. Turn right onto VA 621 when you reach the river. The launch is just a bit farther on the left. (2) *Take-out at Castleman's Ferry.* From I-66 take the U.S. 340/522 exit north at Front Royal to Berryville. Then turn right onto VA 7 and follow until you reach the river. *Note:* To reach the take-out from the put-in backtrack to VA 608 and turn left off VA 7.

Right from the put-in the features on this trip look promising. There are some shallow ledges and riffles that are accessible to wade fishermen, and a large island splits the river directly below them. Probe the cuts and banks along the island's left side carefully— buzzbaits and spinnerbaits can produce some nice strikes through here.

Near the end of the island, on the left side of the river, you will find Watermelon Park (see the appendix, p. 78). This camping/ fishing area on VA 621 charges a fee for entry and also rents tubes and sells bait at the camp store, the Hot Spot. The name is an apt one, as big smallmouth and muskie are caught in the area. I was told by locals that a 43-inch muskie and a 6-pound smallmouth were caught in the vicinity in 2003. A series of Class I rapids lie below the island, followed by riffles that are ideal places to target big fish.

The good fishing continues below this area until you encounter yet another island and more small rapids just before the float's end. The take-out at Castleman's Ferry is on the right, at the VA 7 bridge. All in all, this trip offers good river habitats, with shallow ledges and multiple small rapids that create the long riffles fish love.

Appendix: Information and Resources

Camping

George Washington National Forest
Lee Ranger District
109 Molineu Road
Edinburg, VA 22824
(540) 984-4101
www.southernregion.fs.fed.us/gwj/lee/forest/recreation/camping/
index.shtml (for information on campgrounds and campsites)

Gooney Creek Campgrounds
7122 Stonewall Jackson Highway
Front Royal, VA 22630
(540) 635-4066

Low Water Bridge Campground
192 Panhandle Road
Bentonville, VA 22610
(540) 635-7277
www.lowwaterbridge.com

Luray Jellystone Park
2250 U.S. Highway 211 East
Luray, VA 22835
(800) 420-6679
www.campluray.com

Riverside Camping
4298 U.S. Highway 340
Shenandoah, VA 22849
(540) 652-1075
www.riversidecampingcanoeing.com

Shenandoah National Park
3655 U.S. Highway 211 East
Luray, VA 22835-9036
(540) 999-3500
www.nps.gov/shen/1b1.htm (for a list of campgrounds)

Shenandoah River State Park (Raymond R. "Andy" Guest Jr.)
P.O. Box 235
Daughter of Stars Drive
Bentonville, VA 22610
(540) 622-6840, (800) 933-PARK (7275)
www.dcr.state.va.us/parks/andygues.htm
shenandoahriver@dcr.state.va.us

Watermelon Park
3322 Lockes Mill Road
Berryville, VA 22611
(540) 955-4803

Fishing Regulations

Virginia Department of Game and Inland Fisheries (VDGIF)
Region IV (Northwest) Office
127 Lee Highway
P.O. Box 996
Verona, VA 24482
(540) 248-9360
www.dgif.state.va.us (main VDGIF website)

Guides, Liveries, and Outfitters

Blue Ridge Angler
1756 South Main Street
Harrisonburg, VA 22801
(540) 574-FISH (3474)
www.blueridgeangler.com

Down River Canoe Company
P.O. Box 10
884 Indian Hollow Road
Bentonville, VA 22610
(800) 338-1963
www.downriver.com

Front Royal Canoe Company
P.O. Box 473
Front Royal, VA 22630
(800) 270-8808
www.frontroyalcanoe.com

Greasy Creek Outfitters
P.O. Box 211
Willis, VA 24380
(540) 789-7811
www.greasycreekoutfitters.com

Long's Outfitters
3095 U.S. Highway 211 East
Luray, VA 22835
(540) 743-7311 or (866) 422-6637
www.longsoutfitters.com

Lou's Guide Service
127 North Jefferson Street
Staunton, Virginia 24401
(540) 255-4923
www.courtrules.org/lousguide

Massanutten River Adventures
1822 Resort Drive
McGaheysville, VA 22840
(540) 289-4066
www.canoe4u.com

Mossy Creek Fly Shop
40 Pine Ridge Lane
Mt. Solon, VA 22843
(800) 646-2168
www.mossycreek.com

Mossy Creek Lodge
5820 Mossy Creek Road
Bridgewater, VA 22182
(540) 867-5252
www.mossycreeklodge.com

Murray's Fly Shop
121 Main Street
P.O. Box 156
Edinburg, VA 22824
(540) 984-4212
www.murraysflyshop.com

River Rental Outfitters
352 Shenandoah Heights Drive
Front Royal, VA 22653
(800) 727-4371

Shenandoah Lodge and Outfitters
100 Grand View Drive
Luray, VA 22385
(800) 866-9958

Shenandoah River Outfitters
6502 South Page Valley Road
Luray, VA 22835
(540) 743-4159 or (800) 6-CANOE-2
www.shenandoahriver.com

Shenandoah River Trips
P.O. Box 145
Bentonville, VA 22610
(800) RAPIDS-1 (727-4371)
www.shenandoah.cc or www.riverrental.com

Smalljaw Guides
219 Spring Lane
Massanutten, VA 22840
(540) 289-6917
egasdyl1@aol.com

Thornton River Fly Shop
P.O. Box 530
Sperryville, VA 22740
(540) 987-9400
www.thorntonfly.com

Village Store Canoeing
10603 Port Republic Road
P.O. Box 36
Port Republic, VA 24471
(540) 249-3096

Wolfs Minnow Bucket
1 Lake Frederick Drive
White Post, VA 22663
(540) 869-1104

Lodging/Dining Information

Front Royal/Warren County Chamber of Commerce
305 East Main Street
Front Royal, VA 22630
(540) 635-3185
www.frontroyalchamber.com

Harrisonburg-Rockingham Chamber of Commerce
800 Country Club Road
Harrisonburg, VA 22802
(540) 434-3862
www.hrchamber.org

Luray–Page County Chamber of Commerce
46 East Main Street
Luray, VA 22835
(888) 743-3915
www.luraypage.com

Shenandoah Valley Travel Association/Tourist Information Center
P.O. Box 1040
New Market, VA 22844
Note: The Tourist Information Center is located at exit 264 off I-81
in New Market
(540) 740-3132
www.visitshenandoah.org

Maps

DeLorme's *Virginia Atlas and Gazetteer*, 4th edition, (Yarmouth, Maine: DeLorme, 2000). ISBN 0-8993-3326-5. Widely available at bookstores and online sources, or see www.delorme.com (DeLorme, Two DeLorme Drive, P.O. Box 298, Yarmouth, ME 04096, (800) 561-5105) for information

Down River Canoe Company
P.O. Box 10
884 Indian Hollow Road
Bentonville, VA 22610
(800) 338-1963
www.downriver.com (see the link for river maps)

Front Royal Canoe Company
P.O. Box 473
Front Royal, VA 22630
(800) 270-8808
www.frontroyalcanoe.com

The Shenandoah River Atlas, by Wm. E. Trout III. Available from the Virginia Canals and Navigations Society, 6826 Rosemont Drive, McLean, VA 22101
http://organizations.rockbridge.net/canal/default.htm (see the link for VC&NS publications)

Shenandoah River Outfitters
6502 South Page Valley Road
Luray, VA 22835
(540) 743-4159 or (800) 6-CANOE-2
www.shenandoahriver.com/entrance.html (see the link for the river
map)

Shenandoah River Trips
P.O. Box 145
Bentonville, VA 22610
(800) RAPIDS-1 (727-4371)
www.shenandoah.cc or www.riverrental.com (see the link for the
river maps)

Virginia Department of Game and Inland Fisheries (VDGIF)
Region IV (Northwest) Office
127 Lee Highway
P.O. Box 996
Verona, VA 24482
(540) 248-9360
Note: Shenandoah River Float Trips is available from the VDGIF,
and maps of both Lake Frederick and Lake Shenandoah can be
found on the website (at www.dgif.state.va.us/fishing/lakes/
lake_frederick/map.html and www.dgif.state.va.us/fishing/
lakes/lake_shenandoah/map.html, respectively)

Parks

George Washington National Forest
Lee Ranger District
109 Molineu Road
Edinburg, VA 22824
(540) 984-4101
www.southernregion.fs.fed.us/gwj/lee/index.shtml

Shenandoah National Park
3655 U.S. Highway 211 East
Luray, VA 22835-9036
(540) 999-3500
www.nps.gov/shen/

Shenandoah River State Park (Raymond R. "Andy" Guest Jr.)
P.O. Box 235
Daughter of Stars Drive
Bentonville, VA 22610
(540) 622-6840, (800) 933-PARK (7275)
www.dcr.state.va.us/parks/andygues.htm
shenandoahriver@dcr.state.va.us

Index

Page references to photographs are in boldface